INCREDIBLE INVENTORS

GEORGE WASHINGTON CARVER AND PEANUT PRODUCTS

BENJAMIN PROUDFIT

Gareth Stevens PUBLISHING

Please visit our website, www.garethstevens.com. For a free color catalog of all our high-quality books, call toll free 1-800-542-2595 or fax 1-877-542-2596.

Cataloging-in-Publication Data

Names: Proudfit, Benjamin, author.
Title: George Washington Carver and peanut products / Benjamin Proudfit.
Description: New York : Gareth Stevens Publishing, [2023] | Series: Incredible inventors | Includes index.
Identifiers: LCCN 2021036673 (print) | LCCN 2021036674 (ebook) | ISBN 9781538276549 (set) | ISBN 9781538276556 (library binding) | ISBN 9781538276532 (paperback) | ISBN 9781538276563 (ebook)
Subjects: LCSH: Carver, George Washington, 1864?-1943–Juvenile literature. | African American agriculturists–United States–Biography–Juvenile literature. | Agriculturists–United States–Biography–Juvenile literature. | Peanuts–Juvenile literature.
Classification: LCC S417.C3 P76 2023 (print) | LCC S417.C3 (ebook) | DDC 630.92 [B]–dc23
LC record available at https://lccn.loc.gov/2021036673
LC ebook record available at https://lccn.loc.gov/2021036674

Published in 2023 by
Gareth Stevens Publishing
111 East 14th Street, Suite 349
New York, NY 10003

Designer: Rachel Rising
Editor: Kristen Nelson

Photo credits: Cover, pp. 1 Johnston, Frances Benjamin,/Libary of Congress; pp. 3-24 Zavadskyi Ihor/Shutterstock.com; pp. 3-24 Lukasz Szwaj/Shutterstock.com; p. 5 Johnston, Frances Benjamin/Libary of Congress; p. 7 MM_photos/Shutterstock.com; pp. 9, 19 Everett Collection/Shutterstock.com; p. 11 Phillip Minnis/Shutterstock.com; p. 13 Ricardo Ninin/Shutterstock.com; p. 15 Ivan Galashchuk/Shutterstock.com; p. 17 Sergiy Akhundov/Shutterstock.com; p. 20 Alexandr Liogkih/Shutterstock.com.

Printed in the United States of America

CONTENTS

Boldface words appear in the glossary.

Early Life

George Washington Carver made important **contributions** to farming and science in the United States. He was born around 1864 in Missouri. Though he was born an **enslaved** person, **slavery** ended in Missouri in 1865. He spent a lot of time learning about plants as a child.

Around age 12, George left home to go to school. He studied music and art. In 1891, he became the first Black American to go to what is now Iowa State University. He studied plants. George started teaching there when he finished school.

32
USA
George Washington Carver
1998
7

Teaching in Tuskegee

Booker T. Washington, founder of the Tuskegee Normal and Industrial Institute, asked George to come work at his school in 1896. Tuskegee was a college for Black students. George said yes. He moved to Alabama to teach and study **agriculture**.

BOOKER T. WASHINGTON

King Cotton

At Tuskegee, George studied peanuts, soybeans, and sweet potatoes. He found crops like these helped keep soil healthier. At the time, farmers in the South grew a lot of cotton. Over time, it had harmed the soil in their fields.

COTTON FIELD

George told farmers to **alternate** growing crops such as peanuts and corn with cotton in their fields. This idea is called crop rotation. Then, in 1914, the **boll weevil** was ruining cotton crops in Alabama. Farmers needed money. They planted peanuts but then needed to sell what they'd grown!

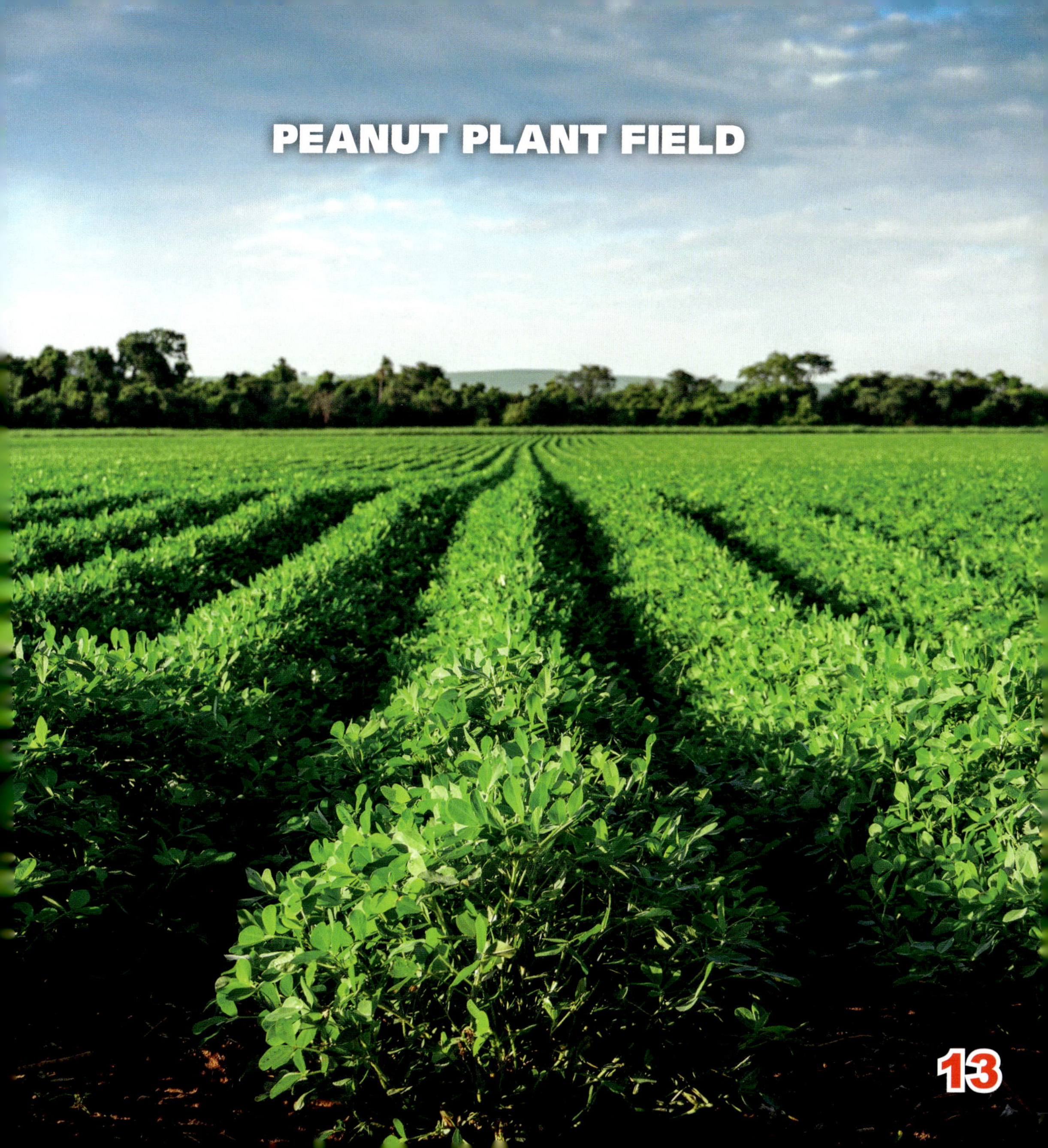
PEANUT PLANT FIELD

From Soup to Nuts

George helped save many farms by coming up with ways to use the peanut crop. He **developed** peanut flour, coffee, and candy. He didn't invent peanut butter, but he made it **popular**. In all, he came up with more than 300 peanut products!

PEANUT FLOUR

Not all his peanut inventions were for eating. He used peanuts to make shampoo, shaving cream, and soap! In addition, George came up with more than 100 ways to use sweet potatoes. He invented sweet potato paper, paint, and even **medicine**.

SWEET
POTATO
PLANT

A Helping Life

George believed in helping others. He made a **mobile** classroom called the Jesup Wagon. George taught poor farmers about crop rotation and the many uses of peanuts, soybeans, and sweet potatoes. His work helped them better feed their families.

Honored

George Washington Carver died on January 5, 1943. His contributions to farming in the South were so great that he was honored with the George Washington Carver National Monument in Missouri. It made him the first Black American to have a national park named for him.

TIMELINE

Around 1864
George Washington Carver is born an enslaved person.

1865
Slavery ends in Missouri.

1891
George begins college at what is now Iowa State University.

1896
He is asked to work at the Tuskegee Normal and Industrial Institute.

1914
The boll weevil harms Alabama cotton crops

1916
George shares what he's learned about how to grow and use peanuts.

January 5, 1943
George Washington Carver dies.

July 14, 1943
George Washington Carver National Monument is established.

GLOSSARY

agriculture: the science or job of farming

alternate: to do different things in a repeating order so that one follows another

boll weevil: a small bug that eats cotton plants

contribution: something that is done to cause something to happen

develop: to create over time

enslaved: having to do with being owned by another person and forced to work without pay

popular: liked by many people

medicine: a drug taken to make a sick person well

mobile: able to move from one place to another

slavery: the state of being owned by another person and forced to work without pay

FOR MORE INFORMATION

BOOKS

Jovin, Michelle. *Fantastic Kids: George Washington Carver.* Huntington Beach, CA: Teacher Created Materials, 2018.

Marsico, Katie. *George Washington Carver.* Ann Arbor, MI: Cherry Lake Publishing, 2019.

WEBSITES

Black Scientists and Inventors
kids.nationalgeographic.com/science/article/black-inventors-and-pioneers-of-science
Find more Black inventors and scientists in this article for kids.

George Washington Carver
kids.nationalgeographic.com/history/article/george-washington-carver
Check out more about George Washington Carver's life here.

Publisher's note to educators and parents: Our editors have carefully reviewed these websites to ensure that they are suitable for students. Many websites change frequently, however, and we cannot guarantee that a site's future contents will continue to meet our high standards of quality and educational value. Be advised that students should be closely supervised whenever they access the internet.

INDEX